A-Z OF
NORFOLK WINDMILLS

A-Z OF
NORFOLK WINDMILLS

MIKE PAGE & ALISON YARDY

HALSGROVE

First published in Great Britain in 2011

Copyright © Mike Page & Alison Yardy 2011

British Library Cataloguing-in-Publication Data
A CIP record for this title is available from the British Library

ISBN 978 0 85704 101 2

HALSGROVE
Halsgrove House,
Ryelands Business Park,
Bagley Road, Wellington, Somerset TA21 9PZ
Tel: 01823 653777   Fax: 01823 216796
email: sales@halsgrove.com

Part of the Halsgrove group of companies
Information on all Halsgrove titles is available at: www.halsgrove.com

Printed in China by Everbest Printing Co Ltd

FOREWORD

As someone with a longstanding association with mills and milling, I am delighted that Mike Page has now turned his attention to the county's windmills. Norfolk is of course well known for its windmill heritage and this book showcases the great variety of windmill remains still to be found in the county.

Many of the examples included are testimony to those who work hard to preserve this part of Norfolk's heritage. A number of the restored windmills are in the care of Norfolk Windmills Trust. The Trust was established almost half a century ago with the aim of preserving a representative selection of the county's windmills; it currently looks after more than twenty. Help is always welcome; the Trust is largely reliant on grants and donations to fund its work as well as the valuable contribution made by volunteers and Friends.

This book looks at the county's mills from a fascinating new perspective and does an excellent job in promoting the cause of windmills in the county

Bryan Read CBE, JP, DL
Chairman of Norfolk Windmills Trust

ACKNOWLEDGEMENTS

Mike Page would like to thank Seething co-pilots Tim Ball, Brian Barr, Peter Day, Dan Gay and Jonathan Howes. Also Judy Speed and Pauline Young for their assistance with the project.

Alison Yardy would like to thank Mike Page for inviting her to supply the text of this book, Richard Hoggett and Alice Cattermole for their expert technical guidance and map production and also all those with whom she has had helpful exchanges on the subject of mills since she embarked on her dissertation in 2002. These include especially Peter Allard, Keith Bacon, Luke Bonwick, Dirk Bouwens, Jamie Campbell, Barbara Eaves, the late Chesney England, Peter Filby, Sally Gibbs, David Holmes, Simon Hudson, Gareth Hughes, Jerry King, the Ludham Archive Group, Robert Malster, the late Bob Morse, Jonathan Neville, Debra Nicholson, Vincent Pargeter, Nigel Pope, Bryan Read, Amanda Rix, Chris Seago, Richard Seago, Joan Snelling, Anthony J Ward and Tom Williamson.

INTRODUCTION

Norfolk is well known as a county of windmills. In total there are more than 200 sites with some visible remains. Numbers are considerably boosted by the survival of around seventy drainage windmills in the Broads' area, many of which worked into the 1940s.

The mills themselves exhibit variation across the county, not least in terms of their proportions from the smallest corn mill with just three floors, up to the tallest, Sutton Mill, with nine floors. Both Old Buckenham and Stoke Ferry are large mills but as can be seen, strikingly different in appearance. Cap designs too vary across the county – the Norfolk boat-shaped cap tends to be found across the central and eastern parts, with the ogee cap more common in the western third, reflecting a different millwrighting tradition there. Domed and conical caps are found along the north Norfolk coast and south of the county and are probably an earlier cap design.

The relatively late working life and limited amount of residential conversion among the Broads' Mills means their remains survive to illustrate a number of developments in windmill technology. Several of those that survive last worked as the earlier manual type of mill which had their cap and canvas-covered 'common' sails hauled round into the wind by the millman. Inside the mills too there is much variety to be found, from an archaic pegged wooden gear in High's Mill, Halvergate, to the fine pitch, cast iron gearing found in Stracey Arms Mill.

There is also great variety in what has become of the mills since they ended work. As will be seen, some are beautifully restored; some remain picturesque derelicts and some are perhaps not immediately recognisable as windmill remains.

Assembling an A to Z (or in fact an A to Y) of Norfolk Windmills is something of a challenge. Mill names are not fixed, some mills are known by multiple names, parishes have been amalgamated and some mills have even moved county. The situation is further confused by the fact that a number of the drainage mills were built in detached parts of their home parish located in the vast triangle of grazing marsh lying between the lower reaches of the rivers Bure, Yare and Waveney.

In general, the alphabetical listing first reflects the place in which the mills were built – with just a few exceptions – the reasons for which are explained in the text.

Alison Yardy
Mike Page

Mill Sites Included in the Text

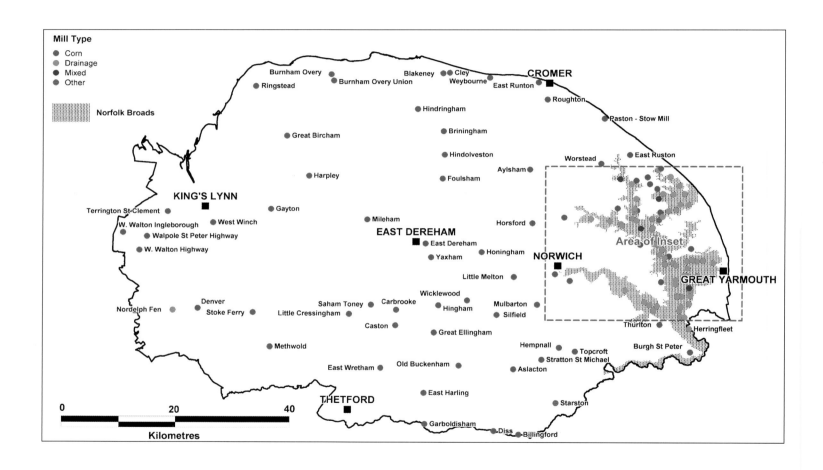

Mill Type
- Corn
- Drainage
- Mixed
- Other

Norfolk Broads

Burnham Overy
Ringstead
Burnham Overy Union
Blakeney
Cley
Weybourne
East Runton
CROMER
Roughton
Paston - Stow Mill
Hindringham
Briningham
Great Bircham
Hindolveston
Worstead
East Ruston
Harpley
Foulsham
Aylsham
KING'S LYNN
Terrington St Clement
Gayton
Mileham
Horsford
Area of Inset
W. Walton Ingleborough
West Winch
EAST DEREHAM
Walpole St Peter Highway
East Dereham
Honingham
NORWICH
W. Walton Highway
Yaxham
GREAT YARMOUTH
Little Melton
Wicklewood
Denver
Saham Toney
Carbrooke
Mulbarton
Nordelph Fen
Stoke Ferry
Little Cressingham
Hingham
Silfield
Caston
Thurlton
Herringfleet
Great Ellingham
Hempnall
Topcroft
Burgh St Peter
Methwold
Stratton St Michael
East Wretham
Old Buckenham
Aslacton
THETFORD
East Harling
Starston
Garboldisham
Diss
Billingford

0   20   40
Kilometres

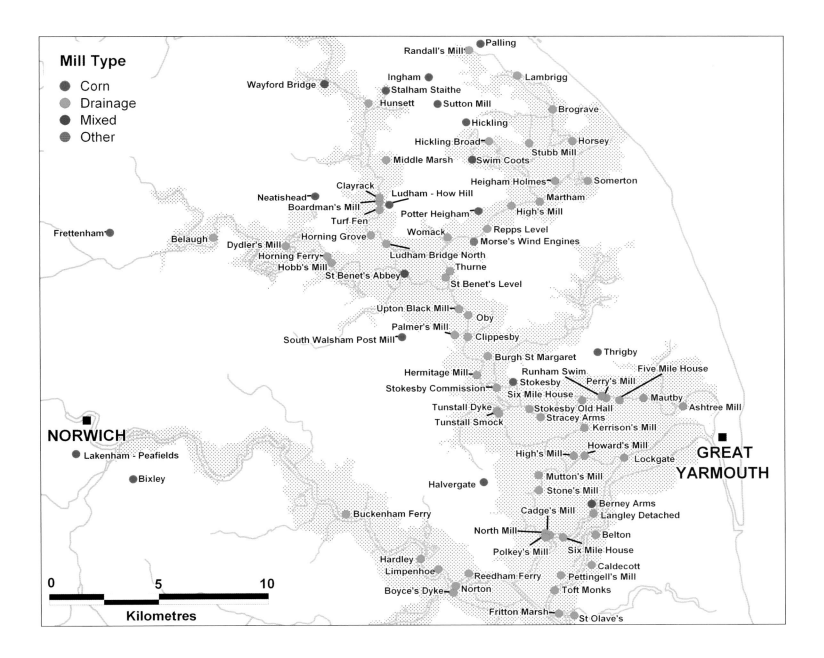

Mill Type

- Corn
- Drainage
- Mixed
- Other

Palling
Randall's Mill
Lambrigg
Ingham
Stalham Staithe
Wayford Bridge
Hunsett
Sutton Mill
Brograve
Hickling
Hickling Broad
Horsey
Stubb Mill
Middle Marsh
Swim Coots
Heigham Holmes
Somerton
Clayrack
Martham
Neatishead
Ludham - How Hill
Boardman's Mill
High's Mill
Turf Fen
Potter Heigham
Repps Level
Womack
Frettenham
Horning Grove
Morse's Wind Engines
Belaugh
Dydler's Mill
Horning Ferry
Ludham Bridge North
Hobb's Mill
Thurne
St Benet's Abbey
St Benet's Level
Upton Black Mill
Oby
Palmer's Mill
South Walsham Post Mill
Clippesby
Burgh St Margaret
Thrigby
Hermitage Mill
Runham Swim
Five Mile House
Stokesby
Perry's Mill
Stokesby Commission
Six Mile House
Mautby
Tunstall Dyke
Stokesby Old Hall
Ashtree Mill
Tunstall Smock
Stracey Arms
Kerrison's Mill
Howard's Mill
High's Mill
Lockgate
NORWICH
GREAT
YARMOUTH
Lakenham - Peafields
Mutton's Mill
Bixley
Stone's Mill
Halvergate
Berney Arms
Cadge's Mill
Langley Detached
Buckenham Ferry
North Mill
Belton
Polkey's Mill
Six Mile House
Caldecott
Hardley
Pettingell's Mill
Limpenhoe
Reedham Ferry
Toft Monks
Boyce's Dyke
Norton
Fritton Marsh
St Olave's

0   5   10

Kilometres

9

ASHTREE FARM MILL

Photographed during river bank re-profiling and piling works on the River Bure in 2010. This mill was one of the last to be built in the Broads (1911–12). It was built by Smithdales of Acle on a restricted budget with much material reused from other mills but with some innovative use of cast iron too. It was also one of the last mills to work. Mr Banham, the marsh farmer, continued to use it even after diesel and electric pumps had been installed nearby. It finally ended work when the sails were torn off in the gales that triggered the 1953 east coast floods. Fifty years on, it was restored 2003 to 2006 by millwright Richard Seago as part of the Norfolk Windmills Trust's 'Land of the Windmills' project.

ACLE – HERMITAGE
This former mill tower was truncated and converted into part of an engine house by Smithdales of Acle.

ACLE – KERRISON'S

Both Kerrison's and Ashtree Farm mills were built to drain marshland on detached outlying parts of Acle parish. This mill appears on the 1799 Acle enclosure map and, although it was modernised in the late nineteenth century, it still contains an early cap frame that has been adapted to carry the later patent sails. Norfolk Windmills Trust have repaired the mill with a static cap to preserve the fragile tower and early cap remains.

ASLACTON
The site under new ownership in 2010. Aslacton Mill last worked by wind in the 1920s.

AYLSHAM

The sails were blown off this mill around 1920. This often resulted in the top of the tower being damaged by the large brakewheel, although tradition has it that this tower was so solidly built that demolition was started but abandoned. Either way, the uneven top has been preserved as a feature. The tower is now managed as holiday accommodation.

BELAUGH

The tower of a small drainage mill is just visible under the vegetation.

BELTON

Belton Black Mill is one of the four mills included in this book that were built in Suffolk, until 1974 boundary changes moved them into Norfolk. The mill is a late re-build of the older manual type of mill – turned into the wind by a long braced tail-pole and fitted with canvas covered common sails. The brick tower is a convex shape presumably reflecting some rapid adjustment by the bricklayer as he neared the required height.

BILLINGFORD

The present mill was built in late 1859/60 after the dramatic collapse of a post mill on this site. It worked for almost 100 years, latterly with just one pair of sails and became the last mill to work by wind in the county. The mill is now in the care of Norfolk Windmills Trust and opened by local volunteers.

Opposite: **BIXLEY**

Built in 1838, this mill was once an extraordinary size – amongst the tallest ever built. It was also relatively short lived, working for around 27 years before the tower was reduced and capped off at a still impressive seven storeys.

BLAKENEY

Technically 'Blakeney' Mill lies just over the parish boundary in neighbouring Wiveton but it forms part of the Friary Farm estate in Blakeney, now owned by the National Trust. The mill contains early wooden gearing and is one of the county's few eighteenth-century windmill survivals, albeit one hidden away in a static caravan park.

BRININGHAM

The lower, octagonal part of this tower was the base of a smock mill built in 1721 and possibly the earliest windmill remains in the county. The timber 'smock' that sat on this base was dismantled in the late eighteenth century and the cylindrical top added to form a viewing tower for the Astley family, owners of the Melton Constable estate.

BUCKENHAM FERRY

The Buckenham Marshes were once part of the Proctor Beauchamp family's Langley estate. This is an early mill site and the present tower has seen a number of alterations. The mill tower was painted white, much like Thurne Mill. There was once a millman's cottage beside the mill as well as a steam engine house.

Left: **BUCKENHAM FERRY – THE RIVER YARE**

Until the 1930s, a long established ferry crossed from The Beauchamp Arms to a landing place upriver on the Buckenham side of the Yare. There was once an inn known as the Three Horse Shoes on the Buckenham side of the river. It was converted into cottages in the 1870s but has long since been demolished.

21

BURGH ST MARGARET

This once fine looking drainage mill was extended and converted into a house in the early 1960s for the television actor John Glyn-Jones. It later became a restaurant and more recently a bed and breakfast and holistic retreat.

BURGH ST PETER

This mill was once a five storey tower with long ten-bay sails. The tower was reduced in height in 1953 and the remains have been converted into a house with rendered walls in recent years.

BURNHAM OVERY

One of the well known Norfolk coastal landmarks. It is owned by the National Trust, along with the nearby watermill, and both now contain accommodation.

BURNHAM OVERY UNION

Burnham Overy was clearly a very popular location for milling. At this site, built by Thomas Beeston in 1814, the mill and watermill were linked together on each floor and known as the Union Mills.

CANTLEY – SIX MILE HOUSE

This mill is in fact located on a detached block of Cantley Marshes on the River Bure, some distance away from Cantley village. The name marks the approximate number of miles by river from Great Yarmouth and is one of a series of Mile House markers that were found along the Rivers Bure, Yare and Waveney.

25

CARBROOKE
Carbrooke is an interesting mid nineteenth century mill that retains its internal machinery. It once had a modern wind generator fitted to the roof.

CASTON

This tall mill and former granary was the base of the late John Lawn, millwright, who worked on many of the mills in this book. The mill dates from 1864 and was built for miller Edward Wyer.

CATFIELD – MIDDLE MARSH
This mill was built in connection with the parliamentary enclosure of Catfield but drainage had been abandoned here by the end of the nineteenth century and the mill is now surrounded by reed beds.

CATFIELD – SWIM COOTS

Although still within the parish of Catfield, this mill lies on the edge of Hickling Broad and was accessed from Potter Heigham. According to Rex Wailes this was a combined corn/drainage windmill. The scoopwheel is located within the tower so it is rather difficult to imagine how this combined with any milling activity, especially in such a small mill.

CHEDGRAVE – SIX MILE HOUSE

Another of the 'Mile House' mills, located on the River Yare on what was a detached block of Chedgrave marshland and one of the four surviving 'Haddiscoe Island' windmills. This mill has unfortunately become marooned in the course of the ongoing flood alleviation works on the River Yare.

CLEY

One of Norfolk's best known mills. Cley Mill was converted to a holiday home in the 1920s. It featured in the 1954 film *Conflict of Wings* starring John Gregson and Muriel Pavlow.

Left:
CLEY MILL AND MARSHES

CLIPPESBY MILL AND ENGINE HOUSE

Clippesby Mill on the River Bure is the Norfolk base of millwright Vincent Pargeter. The present engine house replaced an earlier one nearer to the mill. Sale particulars from 1924 reveal that it then contained an 8 h.p. steam engine and turbine and the mill had recently had a new top at a cost of £500.

DENVER
This popular visitor attraction includes the working windmill, holiday cottages, bakery, cafe and shop.

DISS

In its working days, this was a large black mill with a tall domed cap known as Button's Mill or Victoria Road Mill. By 1973, the truncated remains had been rendered and painted white as part of an unusual and well publicised residential conversion. The mill no longer appears to be in use as such.

EAST DEREHAM 2005

EAST DEREHAM 2010

Despite its restoration in the 1980s, and the best efforts of the mill's Friends group to secure recent funding, Dereham Mill has once again fallen on hard times. The remains of the sail frames have recently been removed.

EAST RUNTON

A new cap and fantail have been fitted in recent years as part of the residential conversion of this mill.

Left: EAST HARLING

The cap visible on the ground in the top left of the picture was made in the 1970s utilising part of the old cap frame and the windshaft from Topcroft Post Mill. It has been fitted on to a low brick base to preserve the remains. A replacement cap is in preparation.

EAST RUSTON
East Ruston was one of the last corn mills in Norfolk to work by windpower.

EAST WRETHAM

In 1875, East Wretham mill was described as 'newly erected' making it one of the last few corn windmills to be built in the county. The tower now forms part of a rather unusual residence.

FOULSHAM

The truncated remains of Foulsham Mill. In its working days, this mill contained six floors and three pairs of millstones with another two pairs driven by steam and later by oil engines. The mill was burnt out within the space of an hour in June 1912. The *Dereham and Fakenham Times* reported that the sails came down with a tremendous crash, though luckily missing the engine house adjoining the mill.

FREETHORPE – LOCKGATE

Also known as Breydon North Wall and Banham's Black Mill. This tall mill was built by Smithdales, then of Norwich, in the 1870s. The remains of one wall of the millman's cottage can be seen to the north of the mill. The mill was last operated by Leonard Carter in the mid 1940s.

FRETTENHAM

Late built c.1880 and according to Harry Apling only working until around 1900. A very rare photograph of the mill with its cap suggests the windshaft may have broken. A new cap has been made for the mill in recent years and the Mill Farm complex converted to residential use.

FRITTON MARSH

Fritton Marsh Mill is a small drainage mill on the River Waveney and before 1974 located in Suffolk. Broads Authority funded restoration work commenced in the 1990s but ended prematurely leaving the mill with this strange looking temporary top.

FRITTON – CALDECOTT

Caldecott is another mill that was formerly in Suffolk. Until the 1990s, although in poor condition, the mill was internally complete with early wooden gearing. A protective aluminium cap was fitted in the 1990s but within a few months the mill suffered an arson attack which gutted the interior. A further attempt to restore the mill was also abandoned after the then owners went into receivership.

GARBOLDISHAM

Norfolk's historic post mill remains are now sadly only fragmentary. The only genuinely old post mill left in the county is this one in Garboldisham which survives thanks to Adrian Colman, who brought the mill back from its long term derelict state in the 1970s and 1980s.

GAYTON
This tall mill finished working by wind in the 1910s. It now forms part of a residential care home complex.

GREAT BIRCHAM
Great Bircham was rescued from dereliction by the Wagg family. The windmill now forms the centrepiece of a visitor attraction that includes a bakery, tea rooms, and accommodation.

GREAT ELLINGHAM
Great Ellingham Mill pictured undergoing conversion and the construction of a large timber extension in 2010.

HALVERGATE

The demise of many a mill was following a 'tail winding' when strong winds and sudden changes in wind direction led to the sails of the mill turning backwards and the brake either unable to hold, or the friction created causing it to catch fire. Halvergate corn mill was burnt out after a tail winding in 1935 when the locals were busy celebrating the King's Jubilee. A new cap made in the 1990s still awaits fitting.

HALVERGATE – HIGH'S MILL

High's Mill is one of a surprising number of Broads' mills that last worked (in this case into the 1940s) as the older, manual type of mill – the canvas covered sails were turned into wind by means of a long braced tailpole (see Herringfleet for the only complete example) which was attached to one of a series of anchor points set up around the base of the mill. The long beam that can be seen passing through the cap was braced to the tailpole. Although the brick tower of this mill has been rebuilt, it still contains archaic wooden top gearing.

HALVERGATE – MUTTON'S MILL
This fine mill is the result of many years of careful restoration by local boatbuilders Paul Reynolds and David High. Unusually the scoop-wheel or waterwheel that this mill drives is housed within the mill tower, rather than to one side, so the mill has a larger than average base to accommodate this.

HARDLEY IN 2005

With Steamboat *Banjo* passing by.

HARDLEY IN 2010

The recent restoration works at Hardley Mill were managed by architect Peter Grix and a team of millwrights and volunteers. It is now the third mill on the River Yare to be fitted with sails. The mill is opened to walkers and boaters on a regular basis.

HARPLEY

This tall mill had an ogee cap and unusually clockwise turning sails in its working days but was tail-winded in the 1920s. During the war the Home Guard heightened the brickwork and added an external iron ladder.

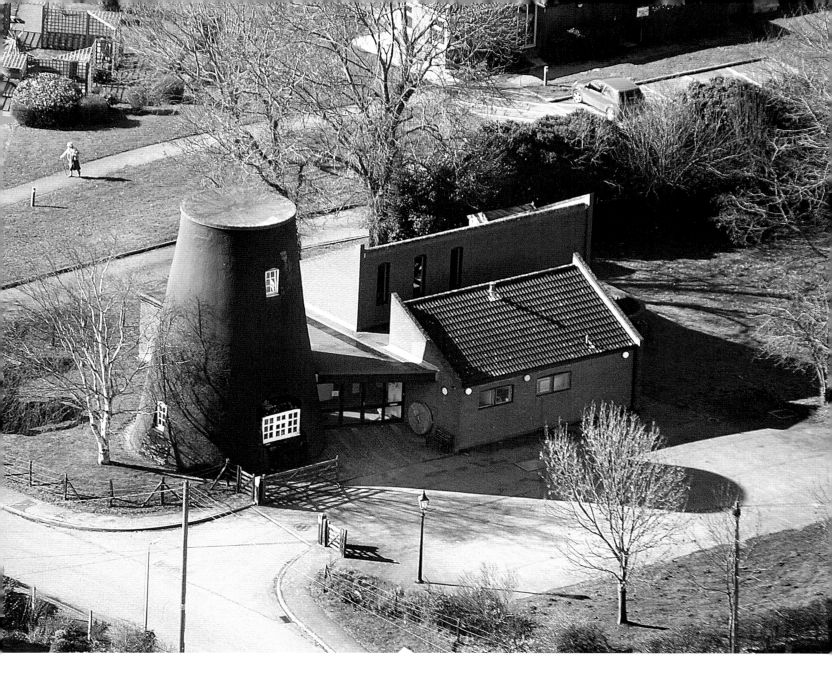

HEMPNALL
This small mill, built in 1814, was converted to form part of a day care centre in the 1970s.

HERRINGFLEET (SUFFOLK)

Not of course in Norfolk but included as one of the finest Broadland mills.

This timber smock mill was built by Barnes of Reedham, probably in the 1830s. By the 1880s it had fallen out of use but it was later put back to work and it worked on into the 1950s. The last millman, Charlie Howlett, continued demonstrating the mill to school parties later still. It is occasionally opened and operated by members of Suffolk Mills Group.

HICKLING

A fine, tall mill still containing much of its wooden gearing and 3 pairs of millstones. It was out of use by the early twentieth century after a working life of almost 100 years.

HICKLING BROAD
Also known as Roland Green's Mill after the renowned bird artist who lived in Hickling for many years and is buried in the churchyard there. At one time he lived on a houseboat and used this former windmill as his studio before building a new bungalow studio nearby.

HICKLING – STUBB MILL 2009

HICKLING – STUBB MILL 2010

Long associated with the Gibbs and later Nudd families. This mill is unusual in the Broads in that it contained living accommodation within the mill tower. The restoration of this important mill was embarked on as a joint Norfolk Wildlife Trust and Broads Authority project for the Broads Authority's Millwrighting Bursary Scheme trainees. The trainee millwrights have restored the mill under the supervision of Vincent Pargeter.

HINDOLVESTON
This mill was built in the 1840s. A dwelling was added to the side of the tower after the mill had finished work in the 1940s.

HINDRINGHAM

Also known as Lower Green Mill, this is a notably low-key residential conversion.

HINGHAM

Hingham mill tower has been truncated from six to three floors.

HORNING FERRY

The Ferry Mill originated as a slender smock drainage mill built in the 1870s or early 1880s by Englands of Ludham for the owners of the Ferry Inn. In 1935 it was transformed into its present form by local firm H P E Neave, although surprisingly, much of the original mill survives within.

Left: HONINGHAM

A small early nineteenth century mill. The mill ceased work in the 1890s. The machinery was removed in the 1970s and the site purchased for development in 1980.

HORNING GROVE

The first of the Broads' mills to be protected with an aluminium cap in 1981. This mill demonstrates the temporary nature of mill names. The stretch of river beside this mill was known to wherrymen as Neave's Reach and Arthur Smith who surveyed the Broads' mills in the 1980s and 1990s called it Neave's Mill. The drainage board have always called it Horning Grove and at other times it has followed the names of the various tenant farmers of Grove Farm – Carman's Mill, Keable's Mill and Tallowin's Mill.

HORNING – HOBBS' MILL

A late nineteenth century skeleton mill slightly taller than Boardman's Mill in Ludham and presumably once operated by a Mr Hobbs.

HORNING – ST BENET'S ABBEY

The bizarre spectacle of a windmill built into the ruins of the abbey gatehouse. This mill seems to have replaced another located in the southeastern corner of the abbey precinct on a map of 1702. It was reputedly built for crushing seeds to produce oil before its conversion to drainage use. The term 'Oilman of St Benets' certainly appears several times in the parish registers. The nineteenth century millman, William Grapes, also kept an inn on the riverside known as The Chequers, the site of which is still visible.

HORSEY

Horsey Mill's location on the B1159 Coast road makes it one of the more accessible drainage mills. The present mill was rebuilt 1911/12 by Englands of Ludham for the Massereene and Ferrard family who owned the Horsey estate at that time. It contains much re-used material from earlier mills on this site. A number of the drainage mills contain small fireplaces; at Horsey there is a small sleeping cabin on the first floor.

HORSEY DYKE

There were two windmills off Horsey Dyke in the early and mid nineteenth century, along with a single storey pair of semi-detached cottages on the site of the present shop.

Left: **HORNING – ST BENET'S LEVEL**

Not many would imagine this mill was in Horning at all, being part of a Ludham estate and closer to Thurne settlement than anywhere else. It is another early site and the tower shows evidence of much alteration. The Hollis family ran the mill for many years in the nineteenth century; they were followed by Charles Wright and later Bob Rice who also operated the ferry that crossed between here and Thurne village. In 1896, it was reported that the mill had been adapted to carry a 40 foot American annular sail. This did not last long as within a couple of years, a traditional cap and sails were reinstated by Englands of Ludham.

HORSFORD

Pictured undergoing part conversion and extension in 2010. The last millers here were the Woodrow family who had milled at Billingford Mill and later Peafield Mill, Lakenham.

HOVETON – DYDLER'S MILL

It is difficult now to imagine this area was ever drained. This tower was converted from a derelict mill in the 1920s into its present form by Drew Miller, author of *Seen From a Windmill* – a book of local tales – and a handbook for visitors *What to do on the Norfolk Broads*. Mr Miller used the glazed top of the tower as a studio to paint in. A dydler is a clearer of water channels in the Broads, taking his name from his principal tool, the dydle.

INGHAM
This mill worked until 1933 and then became part of a Royal Observer Corps post.

INGHAM – RANDALL'S MILL
Once a very tall drainage mill. The tower was cut down to form part of an engine house in the 1930s by Smithdales of Acle.

Opposite: **IRSTEAD – TURF FEN MILL**
Built by William Rust of Stalham and fitted with 2 scoopwheels, one of only three examples known to have been built in the Broads.

LAKENHAM – PEAFIELD MILL

This tall former corn mill was built by millwright Henry Lock in 1824 in what was then a rural location. In 1905 it was purchased by Charles Edward Woodrow. It became part of Woodrow's modern roller milling operation until their 1965 merger with R J Read which transferred the business to Stalham Mills. In 1970, the site was bought by the Norwich Corporation who embarked on conversion into accommodation.

LANGLEY
Known as Langley Detached or Red Mill and once part of the Proctor Beauchamp family's Langley estate, this mill drained the marshes in the northern tip of Haddiscoe Island.

LIMPENHOE

LIMPENHOE DETAIL
The derelict remains of Limpenhoe drainage mill on the River Yare.

LITTLE CRESSINGHAM

Little Cressingham Mill is a combined wind and water mill built originally as part of the Clermont estate. The mill contained two pairs of stones that were powered by the waterwheel beside the tower as well as two more pairs of wind-driven stones. The small white building is a pump house that was used to convey water for use in the gardens of Clermont Lodge.

LITTLE MELTON
An empty brick tower believed to have last worked in 1904.

LUDHAM

Ludham had three corn windmills in the nineteenth century. This one at How Hill was built in 1825 for the Page family, prominent local farmers and millers. The mill house and then derelict mill were acquired by Norwich architect Edward Boardman in 1902. For many years the mill was used as a water tower before its present role as holiday accommodation.

LUDHAM – BOARDMAN'S MILL

A small skeleton mill designed and built c.1897 by the local millwrights Englands of Ludham. These mills were an inexpensive and lightweight alternative found in the Broads from the last quarter of the nineteenth century. Their use was mainly confined to relatively small areas in the upper river valleys.

Opposite: **LUDHAM BRIDGE NORTH**

A small tower mill that had clockwise turning sails. The mill was used as a Home Guard base in WWII and retains its loopholes. A concrete spigot mortar base can also be seen beside the tower.

LUDHAM – CLAYRACK

In the early 1980s, the remains of a hollow post mill was discovered in Ranworth. Norfolk County Council led a project to salvage the remains and rebuild them at How Hill in Ludham. The top and sails of the mill had completely disappeared so the design of these was based on old photographs of hollow post mills at Irstead and Belaugh. The mill is currently awaiting new sails.

LUDHAM – WOMACK
The remains of a tailpole winded mill made redundant towards the end of the nineteenth century. No early photographs of this mill have
come to light.

MARTHAM
Built in 1908 by Englands of Ludham, this was among the last crop of drainage windmills to be built in the Broads. It sported a number of England features including decorative cap gallery, internal turbine pump and a ten bladed fantail or fly.

MAUTBY

This is another eighteenth century drainage mill site. The derelict mill was converted to residential use in the 1980s. In 1919 a Ruston and Hornsby oil engine was installed on the site by Smithdales of Acle. This was salvaged in the 1960s by the late Bob Morse of Repps and for many years was on display in the Fleggburgh Bygone Village museum.

METHWOLD
This was a particularly shortlived windmill. Built in 1875 it probably ended use after gale damage in 1895. The mill tower survives here now as a curiosity within a modern farmyard.

MILEHAM

A derelict tower only: the mill has been out of use since it was damaged in 1918.

MULBARTON
A small three-storey tower that was derelict by 1926.

 NEATISHEAD
A relatively small mill that worked into the
1930s – latterly with one pair of sails.

NORDELPH FEN
The larger of two windmill remains in this west Norfolk part of the Fens. The scale of these mills was vast in comparison with the Broadland Mills clearly having much more in common with the Dutch mills.

NORTON SUBCOURSE – BOYCE'S DYKE
Another of the truncated windmill towers used to form part of an engine house.

NORTON SUBCOURSE

This drainage mill on the River Yare is believed to date from 1863. A new boat-shaped cap has been fitted to this tower in recent years to create a more traditional appearance. The mill has been converted into holiday accommodation.

OBY

This mill used to display the date 1753 on the tower in metal numerals. It was long associated with the Davey family who at one time also operated neighbouring Clippesby Mill. The sails were taken down in 1933. The timber building adjacent housed firstly a steam engine and later a Blackstone oil engine which were used to power the mill's turbine (centrifugal pump).

OLD BUCKENHAM

The proportions of this tower and lack of batter may suggest the tower was originally intended to be taller. It was fitted with five pairs of mill-stones. Illustrious former owners include J & J Colman of mustard fame and Prince Frederick Victor Duleep Singh. The mill is in the care of Norfolk Windmills Trust.

PALLING
Palling Mill seems to have ended work in the early 1930s.

PASTON – STOW MILL

This well known local landmark was owned by the Gaze family from its construction in the 1820s until 1906. The mill ended work in 1930 when it was cleared of its machinery and converted into an annexe to the Mill House. From the 1970s under new ownership, the mill has been steadily re-equipped with parts of other mills.

POTTER HEIGHAM – HEIGHAM HOLMES

Although this mill is visible from the River Thurne, Heigham Holmes (sometimes called Martham Holmes) is a rather mysterious and inaccessible place. The area is reputed to have been used as a secret WWII landing ground for the black painted Lysander aircraft.

In 1940, the Drainage Board announced that the Martham Holmes mills were to be scrapped. The mill seems to have subsequently suffered impact shock caused by a bomb landing on the marshes nearby which caused the fantail frame to collapse inwards. It was fitted with a protective aluminium top in the 1980s.

POTTER HEIGHAM – HIGH'S MILL

Before the High family arrived to take over this mill in 1924 the mill was known as Grapes' mill having been run by several generations of that family. The mill latterly worked in partnership with a steam engine but this was put out of action in the 1938 floods when salt water entered the boiler.

Left: POTTER HEIGHAM

A fine corn mill built by Martins, the Beccles millwrights. The top is fitted with a conical metal cap but the interior remains intact having been latterly powered by electricity. Harry Apling noted the amount of rather interesting graffiti in the mill including not only the arrival and departure of various millers, the last of which were the Blaxell family, but also the great gale of 1895, the loss of the *Titanic*, and the great flood in 1912.

REEDHAM – BERNEY ARMS

Built as part of a cement works and used originally to grind cement. In 1883 it was converted to a drainage mill by Richard Barnes of Southtown Ironworks. At around 70 feet tall it is easily the tallest of the drainage mills. Sheila and Paul Hutchinson have produced a popular series of local books detailing the history of this area. Sheila's grandfather, Henry 'Yoiton' Hewitt, looked after the mill in its later years. It is now a Scheduled Monument and in the care of English Heritage.

REEDHAM – CADGE'S MILL

Built in the 1870s by Smithdales of Norwich near the site of an earlier mill. The mill ended work around 1941 when diesel powered drainage pumps were installed and the level was joined up to its neighbour. The mill had its scoopwheel housed within the tower, although this now contains the switch gear for the modern electric pump. The new cap was made by Vincent Pargeter re-using parts of the original under the Land of the Windmills project.

REEDHAM FERRY

This mill was extensively modernised by Englands of Ludham in the late nineteenth century. It was gale damaged in the 1920s and later acquired for residential conversion. The conversion proved quite a radical change in appearance from the mill's working days. It is still in use as holiday accommodation.

REEDHAM – NORTH MILL

Built around the 1830s, the mill is in a rather odd position, a long way from the river. It was in the same ownership as Polkey's Mill so may well have been built to assist with the drainage of a low spot on that level. It probably fell out of use after the installation of the steam engine on the level in 1880.

REEDHAM – POLKEY'S MILL AND STEAM ENGINE HOUSE

A fine windmill restored for the Norfolk Windmills Trust by Vincent Pargeter between 2002 and 2005. Vincent found re-used material from a Dutch or Fenland type of smock mill in the floors of this mill. The adjacent steam engine house once contained a large single cylinder horizontal steam engine built in 1880 by Richard Barnes of Southtown Ironworks for John W. Rose of Old Hall, Reedham. Unfortunately this was broken up for scrap in the 1960s.

REPPS LEVEL

A brand new traditional style boat-shaped cap has been fitted to this house-converted mill in 2010.

REPPS LEVEL MILL

REPPS – MORSE'S WIND ENGINE PARK

This group of wind engines were collected by the late Bob Morse (see also Thurne Mill). The collection also includes a small Holmes steam engine, originally used for drainage in Hemsby, and a large open scoopwheel salvaged from a site at Whitlingham near Norwich.

RINGSTEAD

One of the few six-sailed mills that were located in Norfolk. Ringstead retains the cross to which the sails were fixed and much internal machinery.

RUNHAM – FIVE MILE

A notably tall drainage mill. Five Mile House was located between this mill and Perry's Mill.

Left: **ROUGHTON**

Since the 1970s this former mill has found a rather unusual use as the headquarters of the local scout group. The scouts have been known to use the mill tower for abseiling.

RUNHAM – PERRY'S MILL
This small drainage mill powered a turbine pump.

RUNHAM SWIM
This mill was originally earmarked for a protective aluminium cap like the two other Runham mills. However Mr W Watts the landowner decided to pay to have the traditional boat-shaped cap restored. Latterly known as Child's Mill after the last millman to run the mill.

SAHAM TONEY
A tall mill converted into a house in 1948.

SOMERTON
Built by Englands of Ludham c.1898, perhaps rather surprisingly, to provide auxiliary power to a steam engine that was already draining the level.

Left: **ST OLAVE'S**
Late built and one of the very last windmills in the Broads to work. This was a skeleton mill like those in Ludham and Horning but was later weatherboarded, probably in an attempt to stiffen up the rather flexible framework. The mill has a history of gale damage, most recently a rather dramatic tailwinding in the January 2007 gales.

SOUTH WALSHAM

This brand new post mill has been built by millwright Richard Seago very close to the site of a lost post mill and based on a particularly decorative style that was once found in the east of the county (e.g. Catfield, Happisburgh, Panxworth).

Left: SMALLBURGH – WAYFORD BRIDGE

A small mill that was once a combined corn and drainage mill. Visitors in the 1940s have recalled seeing the milling machinery still in situ.

SOUTH WALSHAM – HOWARD'S MILL

This mill is located on Halvergate Fleet on a block of marshland that was part of the parish of South Walsham St Lawrence. It last worked in the 1940s with one pair of sails, before gradually becoming derelict. It was later acquired and restored over a twenty year period by Richard Seago.

STALHAM – HUNSETT MILL

For many years the Hunsett Mill site on the River Ant provided a favoured scene for images of the Broads. The mill was built by William Rust of Stalham probably in the 1860s, replacing an earlier mill on the site. Like Turf Fen Mill, located further down river, Hunsett Mill was unusual for having twin scoopwheels, one at each side of the tower.

STALHAM – HUNSETT LATE 2009

The millman's house has now been stripped of its various piecemeal extensions and has a new architect designed 'shadow' extension. The Wherry *Albion* completes the scene.

STALHAM STAITHE

In the late nineteenth century, this mill, along with a pair of waterside cottages and cluster of reed-covered boathouses formed a favourite scene with all the well known Broadland photographers including Payne Jennings, P H Emerson and George Christopher Davies. The mill, latterly known as Burton's Mill, ceased work in the 1920s and was partially dismantled soon after. During the war it was fitted with a reinforced concrete roof and used as a bomb shelter.

STARSTON
Built by the Suffolk firm Whitmore and Binyon. This little mill powered two plunger pumps that lifted water up from Starston Beck to the home farm at Starston Place.

STRATTON ST MICHAEL

STRATTON ST MICHAEL MODERN MILLING COMPLEX

The windmill ceased work before WWII but is protected with a conical top.

STOKE FERRY

An usually tall and slender tower worth comparing to the stocky proportions of Old Buckenham Mill. Today the mill is used as holiday accommodation.

STOKESBY – CORN MILL
Known as Trett's Mill, the mill worked until 1916.

STOKESBY – COMMISSION MILL

An early mill site. A predecessor of this mill is marked on a 1721 map of Stokesby Common.

STOKESBY – OLD HALL MILL
A former older manual type of cloth-sailed windmill and, unusually, a tiny derelict millman's cottage.

SUTTON
Built in 1862 by Englands of Ludham after a fire at the earlier mill on the site. One of the finest and most (internally) complete mills in the county although currently in a sadly declining state.

TERRINGTON ST CLEMENT
Once a tall tower with six sails, it was cut down to three storeys in 1908 and remains flanked by two former granaries within a once-impressive industrial complex.

THRIGBY

The round house here survives from the original post mill on this site; the remainder is, rather surprisingly, a reconstruction carried out by former owner Nick Prior.

THURLTON
The tower at Thurlton has been reduced in height from its working days and converted to residential use. The sails in the yard were made many years ago for another mill.

THURNE

One of Norfolk's most photographed mills, rescued in the 1940s by the late Bob Morse of Repps, a pioneering conservator of all things mechanical.

Thurne Mill was built c.1820 in association with the Parliamentary Enclosure of Thurne and modernised in the late nineteenth century. In 1919, the mill was tailwinded and the cap and sails crashed rather spectacularly to the ground. They were reinstated but damaged again for a final time in the late 1930s. In recent years the Norfolk Windmills Trust and millwright Vincent Pargeter have completed the restoration of the mill back to working order.

TOFT MONKS – PETTINGELL'S MILL
This small Haddiscoe Island mill last worked by wind with one pair of common sails and one pair of patent sails taken from Caldecott Mill across the river.

TOFT MONKS
Another of the Haddiscoe Island mills. The remains of a Smithdale 'humpback' steam engine lie near the track that passes this site.

TOPCROFT

Any postmill survivals are pretty exceptional in Norfolk now. At Topcroft, the whole substructure – main post, crosstrees and quarter bars – survives.

TUNSTALL – STRACEY ARMS

In many ways this mill demonstrates the final development of the Broads' mills. Built in 1883 by Richard Barnes the Great Yarmouth mill-wright, the mill has all iron gearing and turbine pump. In the war it was turned into a pillbox and it is still possible to see where the loop-holes were. It was presented to Norfolk County Council by Lady Stracey and restored by Smithdales of Acle in the 1960s. The mill is in the care of Norfolk Windmills Trust.

TUNSTALL DYKE

Tunstall Dyke is now dry but must once have been a hive of activity with wherries, cottages, storage buildings, steam engine house and windmills.

Only the windmills survive, the tower mill was apparently burnt out in the 1920s but the pitwheel and scoopwheel were reinstated and driven by an engine.

TUNSTALL SMOCK

This was a late-built smock mill that was subsequently cut down to form part of an engine house. The smock base contains a turbine well. The attached shed contains an early electric motor. No photographs have yet come to light to show what the smock mill looked like in its working life.

UPTON – BLACK MILL AND ENGINE HOUSE

The mill was originally constructed in association with the enclosure and drainage of the Upton Marshes 1800 to 1802. It was heightened and modernised c.1900 by Smithdales of Acle. The engine house originally housed a Robey steam engine later replaced by a Ruston and Hornsby diesel engine which is still in situ.

UPTON – PALMER'S MILL
A small and rare hollow post mill originally located in neighbouring Acle. The derelict remains were salvaged in the 1970s by the then 17 year old Richard Seago and reconstructed over several years near Upton Dyke. The sails can regularly be seen turning.

 WALPOLE ST PETER
Also known as Cooper's Mill, this tower once had an ogee-shaped cap. The sails were in place until 1947.

WAXHAM – BROGRAVE

This derelict shell is a favourite of artists and photographers. Its name relates to the infamous Berney Brograve, a notorious local character who owned nearby Waxham Hall. A date-stone *BB 1771* marks the construction of the mill, although much of what survives relates to a later modernisation.

WAXHAM – LAMBRIGG

Located on Waxham New Cut, although beyond the limit of navigation, this little known mill displays much of interest and along with the Brograve and Heigham Holmes mills retains the timber sail stocks from its working days.

WEST WALTON – HIGHWAY

Probably an eighteenth century tower. The heightening in 1815 for the miller John Dobbs is recorded on a datestone. The mill was fitted with an ogee cap. After its removal, the top of the tower was castellated for many years although this has now been removed.

WEST WALTON – INGLEBOROUGH

Ingleborough Mill was one of Norfolk's few six-sailed mills. The tower is a tall one – eight floors – and it contained four pairs of stones. The tower later became part of Garfoots modern milling complex.

WEST WINCH

West Winch windmill ceased work in the 1920s but the site was not sold by the Kerrison family until the 1970s. It was purchased for restoration by a local builder who carried out restoration works with Lennard and Lawn Millwrights. The cap and sails are currently dismantled.

WEYBOURNE
Another of the well-known north Norfolk coast mills. As with Cley, Burnham Overy and Ringstead, it was acquired for conversion into accommodation in the 1920s.

WICKHAMPTON
Known as Stone's or Kerry's Mill. This is one of the series of mills located along the Halvergate Fleet watercourse. The mill is leaning and inaccessible.

WICKLEWOOD

A mid-nineteenth century windmill. It was purchased by William Wade in 1906. He and his son Dennis were the last to work the mill. In 1977, Margaret Edwards, a granddaughter of William Wade, passed the mill to the Norfolk County Council for preservation by Norfolk Windmills Trust. Much restoration work was carried out by John Lawn in the early 1980s.

The small building to the right of the mill is an engine shed of clay lump construction which once again houses its Shanks paraffin engine from the 1920s after this was tracked down and returned to the site in recent years.

WORSTEAD

Located close to the North Walsham and Dilham canal and latterly operated by Cubitt and Walker who also ran the nearby Briggate water-mill. The mill is now a residential conversion and one of few corn mills to retain the cap from its working days.

WYMONDHAM – SILFIELD
A mid nineteenth century mill, redundant from 1911. The empty tower was converted to residential use c.1980.

YARE NAVIGATION RACE 2010
Windpower is still harnessed today. Seen here driving yachts at speed and turning wind turbines of the Scroby Sands windfarm in the distance.

YAXHAM
Built in 1860, the tower was fitted with an ogee-shaped cap, usually only found in the west of the county. The former milling and bakery complex has been developed into a restaurant and accommodation.

SUNSET OVER BERNEY ARMS

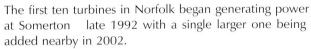

The first ten turbines in Norfolk began generating power at Somerton late 1992 with a single larger one being added nearby in 2002.

On the Ecotech site at Swaffham a large turbine with viewing platform was erected in 1999 with a further one added in 2003.

One of the first offshore windfarms was built on Scroby Sands and by 2004 was generating electricity.

Today larger windfarms each having ninety or more turbines are being built off the Norfolk coast at Sheringham Shoal in the hope that they will provide 'green' energy.

On North Pickenham airfield eight turbines became operational in 2006 whilst a vertical axis turbine, believed to be the first in Norfolk, was erected at Longham in 2010.

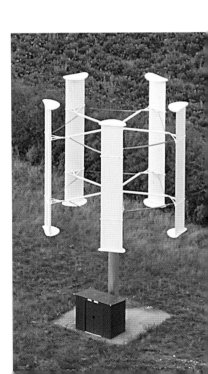

Bibliography/Further Reading

Apling, Harry, *Norfolk Corn Windmills*, (Norfolk Windmills Trust, 1984)
>The key source of historic information on the surviving corn mills.
>Harry Apling's index cards on all known corn mills have now been placed in the Norfolk Record Office.

Bonwick, Luke, *Norfolk's Windmills by River, Road and Rail* (Bonwick Publishing, 2008)
>A very useful introductory guide to a selection of the county's mills with helpful information for visitors. (www.bonwick.co.uk)

Hutchinson, Sheila, *Berney Arms: Past and Present* (2000); *The Halvergate Fleet: Past and Present* (2001); *The Island: Past and Present* (2002); *Berney Arms Remembered* (2003); *The Lower Bure* (2008); *The River Yare: Breydon and Beyond* (2010) (Sheila and Paul Hutchinson)

Malster, Robert, *The Norfolk and Suffolk Broads* (Phillimore, 2003)

Pestell, Tim, *St Benet's Abbey: A Guide and History* (Norfolk Archaeological Trust, 2007)

Silk, Steve, *Wherryman's Way: A Guide to Norfolk's Long Distance Footpath* (Halsgrove, 2010) Steve's blog is: wherrymansweb.blogspot.com

Smith Arthur, C.,
- *Corn Windmills in Norfolk* (Stevenage Museum, 1982)
- *Drainage Windmills of the Norfolk Marshes* (Arthur Smith, 1990)

Wailes, Rex, *The English Windmill*, (Routledge and Kegan Paul Ltd, 1954)

Williamson, Tom, *The Norfolk Broads: A Landscape History* (Manchester University Press, 1997

Yardy Alison and Martin Scott, 'Windmills' in *An Historical Atlas of Norfolk* (Phillimore, 2005)

Yardy Alison, *Mills of the Halvergate Marshes: Reedham Marshes & Ashtree Farm* (Norfolk Windmills Trust, 2008)

Websites

Selected information from Harry Apling's index cards and much more can be found on Jonathan Neville's Norfolk Mills website (www.norfolkmills.co.uk)

The Mills Archive (www.millsarchive.com)

Norfolk Heritage Explorer (www.heritage.norfolk.gov.uk)

Supporting Windmills

National Mills Weekend is the second weekend in May each year. Check the website www.nationalmillsweekend for details of mills nationwide that are open on that weekend and throughout the year.

Join mill support groups such as the Friends of Norfolk Mills (www.friendsofnorfolkmills.org), Suffolk Mills Group and the Mills Section of the Society for the Protection of Ancient Buildings (www.spab.org.uk) to keep up to date with mill news and for details of volunteering opportunities. The Mills Section can provide details of mill support groups for individual mills and those in other parts of the country.

Norfolk Windmills Trust is a charitable organisation administered by Norfolk County Council with more than 20 mills in its care. The Windmills Trust is not a membership organisation but a number of its mills can be visited and you can keep up to date with news of the mills in its care via the Trust's website, (www.norfolkwindmills.co.uk).